Spotting, Coping, Escaping and Recovering from

Narcissists

Love Bombing and Coercive Control

John Smale

AUTHOR OF:
STOP BELIEVING THE LIES, BELIEVE IN YOURSELF

I0087971

i

Published in July 2022 by emp3books Ltd
6 Silvester Way , Church Crookham, GU52 0TD

©John Smale 2022

ISBN: 978-1-910734-50-6

www.emp3books.com

CONTENTS

INTRODUCTION

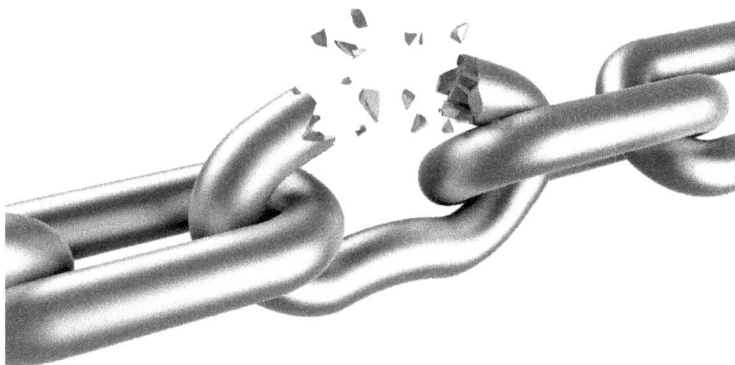

PLEASE NOTE. I will use the word narcissists to encompass NPD or Narcissistic Personality Disorder, coercive controllers and love bombers. They can be male or female but I will refer to them as male because there seem to be more men than women who are involved in these forms of abuse, and it makes it easier to read rather than using he/she throughout.

The words relating to male are used in the generic sense rather than being gender specific. So however you identify, then change the words in the text to suit your own character.

Narcissism is a condition, a mental illness that is independent of gender. So, whichever gender identity the narcissist has, it is always about self-love and the need for others to put them on a pedestal from which they can look down at them and demand subservience.

The casualties of narcissists will be referred to as 'victims', although as you progress through this book, they will be called 'survivors'.

The purpose of this book.
Control by narcissists, love bombers and coercive people is not new, but it is growing in epidemic proportions. It has been accelerated by various factors. The COVID lockdowns, the widespread use of social media and the isolation many people feel in this modern and threatening world.

This book will explain how to deal with two situations. It will help the readers, victims and potential victims to spot the danger before it harms them and, if already caught, how they can escape.

Toxic relationships are called that because they poison not only the victim but all the friends and relatives that they have.

Perhaps, rather than yourself, you might recognise a friend in the trap and need to help them. Sometimes difficult, but also very possible.

I have drawn on advice that I have put into other books. This is important because where the methods for recovery have been already been written, I am happy to share them.

This is a relatively short book because I am aware that it should be for help rather than a huge academic tome that offers little assistance in resolving the big issue of a narcissist in your life.

Nor is it padded out with case studies because you are an individual with your own tale. Reading about others is fairly pointless. This book is about helping you.

My Credentials
I was a therapist with many years of experience in helping damaged people to repair. I want to give insights into how to avoid the predators, and how people who have been caught can escape from the control of the chameleons who disguise themselves to enter and destroy lives.

I saw the destruction that narcissists, controllers and love bombers cause because they have a major fault that, no matter how hard therapists have tried, cannot be eradicated from them, but which presents a major risk for their prey.

My assistance for victims was very successful, if I may

boast, but my pleasure was in witnessing the eradication of misery and the re-emergence of happiness. Now this book gives comprehensive advice about how to recover your life from the hands of the person who stole it.

From conducting those therapy sessions, it became clear that there are very common traits and so I will explain two things.

1. How to spot them and run before they get started.

2. If you have got one, it was not your fault. You were trapped by a devious expert and you need to remove him from your life. It was if you bought a shiny new car but discovered there was a defect. That was there in the beginning. It was not caused by you but you might want to attempt repair. Impossible. Send it back and get a better new one.

As a note to the above, I saw many damaged people, victims, but never anybody who admitted to being a narcissist. They would have only presented themselves in order to claim a victory over me to impress their victim or lied that I had found they did not have a problem. Both of those statements would have been purely to manipulate the truth for their own advantage.

I repeat, rather than wasting your time with long, page filling, academic descriptions about narcissists, love - bombers and coercive controllers, this book is about recognising them but more importantly how to escape and survive to rebuild your life in positive ways.

WHAT IS A NARCISSIST

Narcissus, the Modern Myth

The myth of Narcissus is about the hunter who saw his reflection in the water of a pond. There was a nymph, Echo, who fell in love with him but he rejected her. The more she saw of him then the more she became infatuated with him but he could only love himself.

I will add a possibility to the story. He wanted his reflection to reciprocate his love and when it did not speak to him, when it was impossible for his love to be returned, then he shouted at the water and smacked it to hurt the person who he wanted. It was always himself but he saw the reflection as another person.

In order to keep the image he saw of himself, he frightened away any other creatures, friends and family to preserve his ownership of what he wanted.

He threatened his mirror image, walked away and heard his reflection beg him to return. When it did, then he did the things that he had done at the beginning to attract the image to him again. He let the troubled waters calm down.

Then the need to punish returned and he told the reflection that it was not as good as it had been because it failed to meet his need to be told that he was the most perfect person in the world despite the way he behaved.

So he would walk away and look in other ponds to try again and again to find his perfect partner, one who would tell him how wonderful he was. And again and again the reflections failed.

He refused love from other reflections because he only desired the perfection he saw in himself.

The Narcissus in your life does not have a pond so he stares into you, and others, to find the reflection of perfection in the beautiful man he knows he is. (But we know different.)

Deluded, sad and lonely, this person has to reap his selfish vanity from somebody. Yet, nobody can fully satisfy his needs and he will NEVER change.

And the sad truth is that there is not just one Narcissus, there are hundreds and thousands of them out there hunting for their prey without any feelings for what they catch.

Unfortunately, rather than a modern myth, this has become a modern epidemic.

What Creates a Narcissist?

That is a big question to which the answer is, 'Are we really bothered?' Oddly enough, if you have been caught, then you might be concerned because if you knew why, then you could heal him. Sorry to say, that is impossible.

They exist and so many claims are made by them as to why they are so needy. Yet, they will never admit to being what they are. You will find them as politicians, businessmen, cult leaders, dictators and anywhere where they will feel esteemed for their power. It is very usual, unfortunately, to hear about celebrities, actors, politicians and pop-stars to be brought to book for using their fame to drag people into their lives to abuse them for their own pleasure and ego-feed.

There are also individuals who crave admiration and the sense of having power. They thrive on the control of minds and bodies.

As for people who try to invade your life. They are damaged and need to cause hurt to the innocent they snare. Their actions are based on the need for self-love and their need to be placed on a pedestal. Their victims are there to adore them in return for unreciprocated love.

The more theories you hear or read about him, then the more you will try to find reasons to understand and to forgive him. This works against YOU. His past problems have nothing to do with you and it is virtually impossible to resolve his issues.

He has a psychotic condition and is beyond the reach of

most psychiatrists, so you will never 'cure' him no matter how hard you try and how much he demands your help. What is happening is that he has created a feeling in yourself that you need to help him and you lavish care onto him. That is what he wants, not assistance in getting better. He does not even acknowledge that he is ill.

Where does he come from? He will have tales of being an orphan, being in a children's home, having his parents die when he was young etc. Think of any sad story and he will adapt it to gain your sympathy and to encourage your empathy which of course, he lacks.

This is all about him weaving the story that he had no love when he was young and that is why he needs it NOW, and from YOU. There is little you can do to determine fact from fiction. The story he tells you has one purpose and that is to entice you into his trap.

He is James Bond, he is the hero who every woman he meets falls in love with and expresses that in bed. Yet there is, and can only be, one person who loves him and that is himself.

There are different types of narcissists but that does not matter either, if you have one in your life. Rather than defining them in psychological terms such as covert or overt or one of the other labels, they fall into the behaviour of dominating and parasitic activities which aim to control others for their own selfish benefits.

So, let us talk about helping YOU. The purpose of this book is to assist you in avoiding them or, if you have one, how to cut the rot out of your life.

TIME FOR A BREAK 1

As this has been fairly full-on, it is worth taking a few moments to recap the main points.

1. **He is a devious, self-obsessed emotional and potentially, physical bully.**

2. **He cannot be helped although he will demand your assistance for attention rather than a remedy.**

3. **HE is how HE is now. His past is a story line to get you hooked.**

SPOTTING THE TRAPS

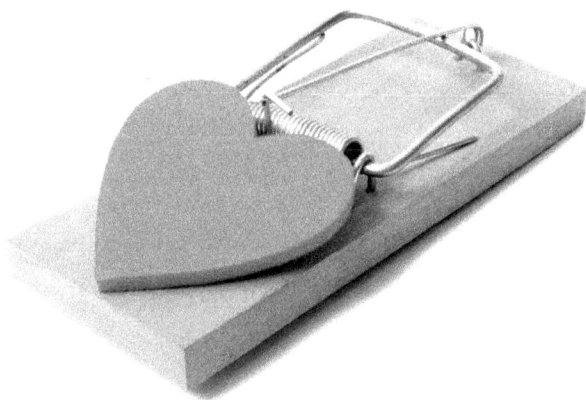

Baited Traps

I HAVE BEEN TOLD THAT I AM NOT ALLOWED TO USE SWEAR WORDS IN THIS BOOK. HOWEVER, THAT DOES NOT PROHIBIT YOU FROM USING YOUR OWN AS ADJECTIVES FOR THESE PEOPLE.

As we are talking about a variety of predators, you will find that I use an assortment of mixed metaphors to make points. Whilst not being perfect in literary terms, they act as illustrations in words.

Lifeforms in nature have the main motivator of finding food. Plants and animals use an incredibly wide range of methods for enticing and catching what will nourish them.

There are the stalkers, big cats and wolves; the sudden attack ones, such as sharks; then the enticers such as the Venus-Fly-Trap that offers nectar and then closes to catch and consume.

In this list we can include parasites that creep in without being noticed at first, the leeches and mosquitoes.

The same wide range applies to the emotional predators.

HUNTER GATHERERS

Narcissists are both. They hunt their prey and then they gather their emotional nutrition from gathering what they need, yearn for, from their captives. The hunt is the intense part called love-bombing which is the plan to trap the quarry

17

by luring them into what is considered a safe place before the consumption of the victim happens. If the captive escapes, then the hunter will start the enticing over again.

Humans have not only the need for nutrition from food, some individuals hunger and crave for emotional nourishment. They also have an incredible armoury for getting it.

Whilst not all people are narcissists, there are enough out there to be cautious about relationships that seem too good to be true.

If you are looking for a partner, a romantic episode or a true love, then there are places you can go to go to, or look at in your search. Yet these places, while seeming safe, can actually be populated with predators. They are the thickets and undergrowth that conceal.

Dating apps are wonderful for finding prey. They are like blood in the water for sharks who are competing in the feeding frenzy for flesh but unlike Jaws, rather than attacking immediately, they will camouflage themselves and pretend that they are the ideal person for you.

They will take their time at first. They will be the perfect gentleman with good manners and then they will start the process of reeling you in.

Intensity is what gets people hooked. His approach will be flattery because he wants you to feel that you have met somebody very special, your soul mate. It is about stealth as the emotionally pleasing words sink in.

REMEMBER, HIS AIM IS TO HOOK YOU.

A magician gets you to believe what he is doing, in order to get you to believe that he is extraordinary and has something to offer that is different to others. It is a trick, an illusion, a deception. Even when you start to see through it, he will try to convince you that he is genuine, the one person in the world who can perform 'real' magic. He will try to convert you to believing he is authentic by performing other tricks. You can call it magic but it is deception, another aspect of love bombing.

Baiting the traps in love bombing.
In every aspect of nature, there are predators and prey. There are two ways to catch the quarry. The first is to hide and when the potential meal is unsuspecting, then the lion, tiger or whatever leaps out, sinks its claws and teeth in and then consumes it.

The second is to entice the victim into a snare and then consume it. Examples are mouse traps, fishing lines with a tempting treat, and then there is the nectar offered by carnivorous plants and so on.

The narcissist will use both methods depending on how he views the person he is tracking.

Camouflage is great for creeping up and captivating somebody. This approach disarms and charms to the extent that the target becomes convinced that she is in no danger, in fact, she has been lucky in finding such a lovely man. Eventually, the wolf in sheep's' clothing will take of the disguise when he needs the captive to return the love he has apparently given. Hunters stalk slowly and strike quickly.

19

This follows the love bombing stage that leads to control and consumption.

The other method is to openly lure somebody into a trap by offering sweetness or sustenance. These are emotional rather than physical things that plants and wild animals use. Something tantalizing is offered which appears to be for the benefit of the recipient but ends in building the marauder's ego and self-love. This might include presents, flowers, promises of holidays. Anything that shows how loving and caring he is. (But he is not.)

In whichever way a person is caught, the user will want to guard the prey to stop it escaping.

The Good Salesmen. In the repertoire of a good salesman, you will find the same techniques that a narcissist uses. They go in stages:

Number one, find the needs of the prospective customer.

Number two, explain how those needs can be satisfied by what is being sold. These are the benefits that the customer will gain.

Number three, gain interest and ask for action or, in other words, a positive response that shows interest.

Number four, the final piece, is to close the sale.

In the terms of a love bomber, he will identify somebody who is looking for companionship and love. Then he explains why he is perfect with so much in common. Then he gets a way of contacting you by phone, message or text. (Now he has locked in your information.) And then a meeting is set up so that he can charm you face to face. The first touch will be light and seductive. The arm, the shoulder, the neck or the face will be important but it will never be more intimate at that point.

Maybe you are feeling so warm towards this 'perfect soulmate, that your usual reserves are put to one side and then a sexual relationship happens. Then you are trapped. You have shared yourself with him and he will start to tighten the noose.

The good salesman is offering the customer something of value. The narcissist is only offering you the chance to idolise him and to feed his need for sycophantic admiration. Yet he needs to pump you up in the beginning. You start to be converted into his tool for his pleasure.

Mirroring. Whatever you like, they will like as well. If you like dogs, they will love them. If you have dogs as pets, they will have had them but do not have any at the moment. Yet they would love to pet yours.

Yet, if you dislike dogs, lo and behold, so does he.

Compliments. At first, they will compliment you for your good looks, your intelligence, your figure. Even talking on social media, they will treat you as if you are as near perfect as you can be. Mind you, he will tell you about his skills and intellect and he will expect you to be impressed.

Contact. They want to be in contact with you at all times by WhatsApp, phone, texts and messaging. This is the start of the control they will need to get you to follow their instructions.

Charm. They will seem to be the most charming person you have ever met. They will be needing your attention all the time in order to praise you.

Time Scale. If you want to eat then it is better when your appetite has grown so it might be a while before you meet him face to face. You will want contact because you have feelings for him. But absence makes the heart grow fonder! Yet once you meet, then speed becomes the main driver.

Speed. Because they have told you so many good things about yourself, the pressure to speed things up will happen. Because you have been caught then you will also feel the need to push ahead with what could, and should, turn out to be you best relationship ever. Your guard will be lowered and your willingness to please will be at its peak and intimacy will happen sooner rather than later.

Soulmates. Because you are so similar, and have so much in common then you are soul mates who have been luckier than most to have found each other. The expression, if it's too good to be true, then it is. Talk to your friends before committing yourself too quickly. Finding a soul mate is a dream; finding a narcissist is a nightmare.

Music. You want to share interests and musical taste is something that soulmates have in common. Never be surprised if he wants you to enjoy his music rather than him sharing yours.

Age difference. If he is younger than you then he has increased his threat level. Women prefer older men so you are lucky to have him. Of course, later on he will then be able to criticise you for showing signs of age and he will tell you that he could easily find a younger partner.

Declarations of love. Falling in love is a slow process. An early declaration of love is a trick to make you feel secure in the relationship and it will speed things up for him. He wants to dominate you to get his rewards. He is impatient and wants his 'fix' of admiration as quickly as possible.

Gentle demands. At this stage demands will be made but they are gently put. If a future with this person develops, beware. They get stronger. 'We will go to the coast today rather than go to your mother's birthday party. Look, you have had lots of birthdays with your mother, but we only go on a trip now and again. Cancel your mum'.

Conversations. Conversations will be one sided. He knows a lot and wants to tell you that he does! He will be an expert in one thing or another and will have to show you, demonstrate what a perfect whatever, he is.

NARCISSISTS AND YOUR MONEY. Not all, but a lot of narcissists will want to control your money. Maybe as a loan to pay for an aunt's life saving operation, perhaps because his investments are slow in paying off. Whatever. He will lie and exaggerate to get his hands on your money and sometimes property. Marriage is a good way to get half a house.

They will want to get more from you than just your devotion.

Be very wary about giving, lending or committing to anything that requires you to outlay your material resources.

Watch this space…more later.

TIME FOR A BREAK 2

As this has been fairly full-on, it is worth taking a few moments to recap the main points.

1. **He works on intensity, compliance, control and demands to get you into his net.**

2. **He, like other predators will, pounce, or stalk and then pounce, entice and/or sneak up to infect you.**

3. **Keep your hands tightly on your purse strings.**

COPING WITH A NARCISSIST

Changing You.
His Tools for Control

**REMEMBER THAT THE ONLY PEOPLE WHO
HIDE THINGS ARE THOSE WITH SOMETHING TO
HIDE.**

A puppet on strings is at the mercy of the puppeteer who decides what the dangling marionette should do. The perfect puppet has had its ability to operate normally depleted by the operator. That is control and that is what the narcissist demands.

Anxiety is a major result of being involved with a controller. It is important to be aware that you are certainly not the only person who has been caught. As there is an enormous number of hunter/predators, so there has to be an equally large number of their victims. You were never a soft vulnerable and idiotic person. You were targeted and caught by somebody whose idea of fun is to dominate and to satisfy a desperate need for attention, praise and sycophancy.

Once he has got his claws into your emotions than it gets more serious. This is what you can expect. These are not set in any particular order; they are the types of things that you will be aware of in part or as a whole.

Empathy. As much as you think you care for him and want to help him out of his problems, he could not give a hoot about you. He is only interested in himself and your issues are of no interest. Whereas you are empathetic, he has no awareness of the meaning of the word.

He has no thought of understanding and sharing feelings with anybody apart from himself. He expects you to comprehend how he feels but will have no interest in your emotional needs.

Your parachutes. In life, we have parachutes. These are there for when we need saving, when we need help. In order for him to control your life and destiny, these need to be changed and at best, removed so that the only parachute you have is your soul-mate. He needs you to depend on him. You need to know that his parachute has strings attached but no canopy.

Family. Your **family** is a danger to him because they know and love you. If they see a big change in you then they can offer support and advice. He will meet your family and once again he will be the charmer who trapped you. They will admire him and be so pleased that you have met up with such a great guy. Then he will find excuses to distance them from you. Dinners and lunches they invite you to will clash with a surprise he has for you. Over time the plan is for them to fade away to be memories rather than people in your life.

The same threat is presented by **friends**. In nature, alpha males fight off competition to gain complete access to the females. A narcissist will demand that you ditch your loyal friends to both avoid rivalry and to stop them from helping you when they see how distressed you are becoming.

It will be necessary in order to please him, to distance yourself and then block them from your life. Who needs friends when he is the best friend you have ever had? Your exit routes have been blocked. There is nobody to talk to or confide in during your darkest moments or when he has threatened, or physically hurt you.

Conversations. As previously mentioned, conversations are controlled by him. They will be one sided. He has knowledge and will impart that to you. You will not be allowed to say too much because your point of view, your activities, your day will be of no interest to him. (Unless he suspects you are not telling the truth about what you have been doing.)

Conditional Love. If...then. Blackmailing you into doing, saying and stating feelings is par for this course. 'If you really loved me, then you would stop seeing your friends, would call me every hour, trust me, would be naked when I get home from work...etc.'

Dress Codes. He will decide what you wear and that will confuse you. He will want you to look sexy, his trophy to show how desirable he is; but he will also want you to hide your figure because he is jealous.

Your appearance. Once again this is one of those contradictory things. Your appearance is as it was when you first met. Now he tells you it has got worse. Your boobs have sagged, your wrinkles are spreading, your backside is too big...or too small. Anything he can do to peck away at your self-confidence will be done. This is because a major part of his character is to be jealous and if he destroys your self-belief then he is protecting himself from loosing his supply of admiration and fawning.

Celebrity Status. Think of celebrities who have abused many people. They did it because they had power. They were able to use their status to intimidate victims into sexual acts through fear. 'Nobody would believe me if I told them'. The use of embarrassment at telling others what was happening was always the most powerful weapon these people used and use to get away with atrocious behaviour.

Remember, he is NOT after you for you. He wants you for him. The love bomber is not after you as the nice individual person, he is preparing you as his 'fix'. He wants to make you vulnerable to satisfy his needs and demands.

Turning 'love' into a drug. He will turn you into a **junkie.** He is one already. He is addicted to loving himself and he needs his supplier of praise to boost him and as his need becomes greater and greater, then he needs his dealer. He needs you to become addicted to him. In this way you will do what he wants in order to make you happy, or in reality, have an illusion of happiness even though there is part of you that is worried at the speed and intensity of what has taken place.

The sculptor. Remember, he wants you to be his reflection. He will chip away to turn you from how you were to what he wants you to be. He wants you to be his sycophant, the person who tells him what he needs to hear. If you do not do that then he will chip bits off that he does not want by threats that range from leaving you to physical hurt. He manipulates.

So, you have been intimate. He has seen you naked and he has had sex with you. I have deliberately avoided the words, made love because love does not come into the equation. He can only love himself.

Part of his sculpting is to change you to please him because you 'love' him. If he shaves his genitals then he will tell you to do the same. If you did before, then he will tell

32

you to grow them.

He will demand sex on his terms, when he wants it, not when you want to. He will like non-involved sex by asking you to pleasure him with oral sex while you receive nothing to please you.

He might ask you to masturbate in front of him, not because it turns him on but because it is a symbol of his control and domination. He fears sex because he has to perform better than your previous lovers, but is unable to.

Cooking. You will do your best to show off your culinary skills and cook the foods he says he likes. You will NEVER match what he has had before. You are not good enough to please him fully. This is the drip, drip, drip becoming a stronger flow that erodes your self-belief and confidence.

Comparisons. Of course, he will have had other girlfriends. Their boobs were perkier than yours. They were not heading south like yours. They had trim tummies and beautiful hair. They were **very** pretty whereas you are **fairly** attractive.

'And I dumped them because they were always suspicious because (I am so perfect) they thought most women would fancy me. Of course, I was never unfaithful. They would not trust me because they were cheats.'

(Can you see Pinocchio's nose growing?)

Trust. People who do not trust see themselves in others. He might very well be a cheat and to protect himself he will talk about people who would not trust him even though he did cheat. By doing this, he is asking for your trust so that when he cheats, he can accuse you of being like the others and he finds it an insult and gets angry with you. Remember, in his head, he is wonderful.

Another part of trust is that unless he can see you or know where you are, his assumption is that you are meeting somebody else. He needs to know your every movement. Only in that way can he prevent another predator from stealing his prey.

Phones. As he owns you then he also has the right to access your phone to check on who you are calling or texting and who is contacting you. He might take the opportunity to plant a tracker on it so he can monitor your every move.

Spying. On the same subject, you might find that your house or apartment has cameras hidden so that you can be watched.

Jealousy. As he knows what he does or fantasises about doing, then he will contain and control you by being jealous. This includes all friends but especially males who he knows, from his own experiences, are all after just one thing. It gives him another threat tactic to prevent you from knowing anybody else but himself. He lives in his own delusional world so he generalises based on his own needs and behaviours.

Stockholm Syndrome. This was the result recognised after a bank raid in Stockholm where people were held as hostages. Those detainees developed a fondness for the captors who were keeping them in confinement. It seems that it is part of our nature to develop positive feelings towards the people who have taken our liberty and is seen in all forms of abuse. After the narcissist has controlled a person over time, then the wish and the ability to escape diminishes. That trap has closed to be watertight. It has its base in self-preservation.

Rejection. Reject before you are rejected is a method for gaining control and maintaining the ego. The love bomber will threaten to walk away or actually do so. This increases the feeling of confusion and helplessness that the victim has. So, she will beg for him not to leave her and promises she will change to be more like what he wants.

When you get to the section about escaping, this is something that YOU can use.

Confusion. Uncertainty, for him, is a neat trick. If you are feeling perplexed, then he has got you doubting your thoughts and suspicions about him. It is always going to be you who gets things wrong. The usual term for this is **gaslighting** whereby you start to doubt your own sanity by being manipulated into believing what is said and done that will create negative thoughts about yourself. This makes you vulnerable which is what is expected of you. He wants you to reliant on him and his needs. You may be lied to or misdirected into not believing the truth about how you are. Again, this is about abusive control.

Ghosting. Another form of the creation of confusing. All contact is shut off and because you have been made to feel dependent on the person who has done it, your feelings of isolation grow. You have no way to make contact so you might blame yourself for doing something wrong and therefore deserve it or you might develop the thought that he has met somebody else who is better than you.

Sadly, he has removed your friends and family so you have nobody to talk to, or so you feel.

Cruelty. The enjoyment of emotional, and sometimes

35

physical pain he inflicts. This is a demonstration of his ability to control by threat.

Stalking. Pursuing somebody is a crime. Remember that these people want to know where you are and who you are with every second of every day, even when you have broken the relationship off and theoretically have no contact. He wants to know if you have replaced him.

STIs. Let us face the facts. He is not the most faithful person on the planet and he is at risk of catching an STI and passing it on to you. Please ensure that you have regular checks and, although difficult, get him to check as well. The problem is that he will angrily accuse you of accusing him of sex outside of your relationship, which if true, he will deny. And **if** true, it makes it imperative that you examine your own state of health.

Hoovering. When you think you have freed yourself, he will want to do his best to get you back, not because he loves you, but because he wants his supply of admiration to be refilled. He will do his best to contact you, promise you the earth and attempt to reset the trap. Once bitten, twice shy. Avoid falling for the honey trap again.

Your thoughts. To show your compliance, you will need to have his thoughts while believing that they are yours. He will do his best to ensure that what he wants you to do is your decision rather than his. Devious mind manipulating is part of his methodology.

TESTING THE WATER
The great question. How would he react if he found you reading this book?

TIME FOR A BREAK 3

That last bit was fairly heavy going so now it is worth taking
another break for a few moments to recap the main points.

1. **He is weak and needs to guard his prey against
    them escaping by control.**

2. **He lacks the fundamental skills of understanding
    and sharing without gaining something for
    himself.**

3. **He needs you to be his mirror image that
    responds positively to him.**

ESCAPING

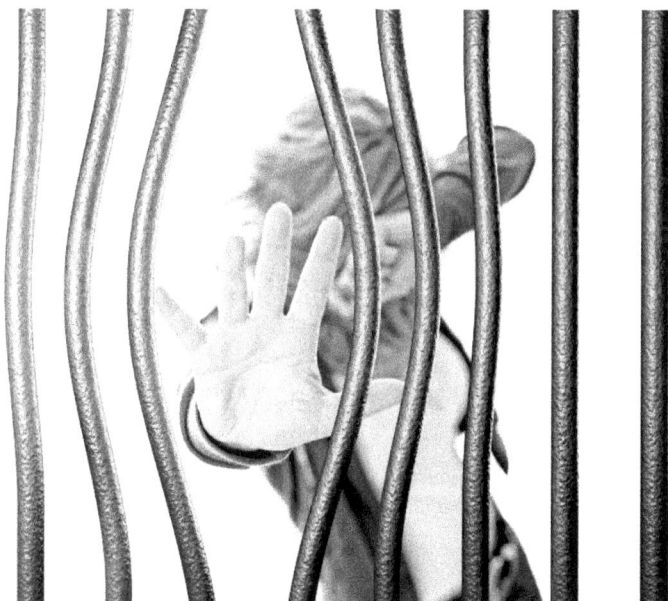

How To Escape

IN TRUTH, THERE IS ONLY ONE SOLUTION.

GET HIM OUT OF YOUR LIFE.

In your heart and soul you know that, but it easier said than done. **This will show you what to do.**

Although it is difficult, it is possible to escape. It will take patience, this never happens in a single day. Expect the narcissist to keep on pushing for his fix. He will never understand why you need your freedom. He has no feelings beyond his own.

So, be determined. The alternative is to continue living a controlled and unhappy existence even though you might miss the artificial highs that he gave you…for his own reward.

There is no magic button that works in one push but think of it as being in an elevator where floor by floor you advance to liberty and happiness.

As much as he wants to impress you with his strength and fortitude, the narcissist is weak rather than strong; and YOU are strong rather than weak.

Knowing unconsciously that they are weak, accounts for why they have to bully and threaten. When you stand up to bullies, they lose their power.

Being aware of, and understanding, his weaknesses is a

necessary piece of wisdom for removing that damage from your life. This takes time and patience but it is worthwhile. It is the key.

Once you have awareness that you are in a toxic relation with one person that spreads like a virus through your other relationships, then it is time to seek safety.

If he is so wonderful, why does he have to pretend, tell lies, scare you, ignore you and try to make you think you are mad?

The simple answer is; despite loving himself, he knows at the back of his mind that he is never good enough to get a partner on normal terms so he has to settle for the only person who loves him, himself.

His weakness is your strength. Once he knows that you know he is weak then it is 'game over'. He will reject you with angry and insulting words because that makes him think he has won when, in fact, he has lost. Those words come from a childish mind having a tantrum.

It is a stark fact that he will never get better. Therapy will fail as certainly as your attempts to help him. He does not want to get better; he wants the disguise of being a lost soul in need of care and understanding as part of his way of closing his grip on the victim even tighter.

The person who **is** able to get better and improve is **you**. You were the innocent victim and you will recover.

As part of the process, **BEWARE** of help groups on social media as they can give your identity away. That makes it possible for you to be targeted by predators who will smell your blood in the water. They can offer to help you and will want to start a dialogue so that they can love bomb in disguise as if they are also victims. The thing they will focus on is your common ground as sufferers and so will start the process of reeling you in. If you want or need to post on those groups, there is no harm in doing so as long as you do so anonymously.

Reject before being rejected.

The one thing he fears above all others is being rejected. Maybe that is why he grew to be as he is, perhaps that is why he bullies in so many different ways. This is a narcissist's Achilles Heel and we will use it.

This is the phenomenon that I used with the clients I saw. I refer to this as 'reject before you are rejected'. This is a self-esteem issue whereby the controller will be lonely because he/she is without friends. They will have been hurt in the past and they adopt the strategy of never committing fully to a new relationship in case they are hurt again. That is why they bully their partner into being dependent. However, if they feel that they are being rejected, then they will push that person away when the relationship develops to the point where he feels vulnerable.

The rescue came from building the client's self-esteem to where they could become able to take the risk of being rejected themselves happening. The fear of that needs to be balanced with the gains. It becomes a 'win, maybe lose, but be happy' situation rather than a 'lose/lose result come what may'. Find the cause of the fear of your rejection and build confidence. If you are being rejected by a control freak, then you will in the lucky position of being freed rather than

43

rejected.

The objective is to use this in order to make the narcissist fear that he is being rejected so that he pre-empts you by discarding you. This equals a win for you.

Ownership. Sometimes after a relationship has ended the narcissist will claim ownership of the other party. Whichever person leaves the house or apartment, they might want to keep a key to enter it whenever they want. The excuse might be to have access to children or a toolkit. This, of course makes new relationships difficult for you, if not impossible. It is continued control. That is why the partner who has left will do it. They are jealous and possessive. They want their cake and they want to eat it as well. It also gives the predator another chance to attempt trapping you. Be firm. Only do what is safe for you and, if vitally necessary, give a key to a trusted person to supervise what is happening while you keep a safe distance.

Part of ownership is having **photos**. These might be to show their success in having caught you by sharing on social media, or as private intimate shots that can be used as blackmail or to show to their buddies after a break up.

We are aware that trophy hunters like to hang heads on the wall or to be photographed with innocent animals they have shot. Your trophy hunter will be seen in the same light and he will be disliked rather than admired.

You need to gain enough confidence to change the locks, take an injunction or other action to stop his interference. I never told a client to do this, my job was to help the client to be strong enough to do it of their own accord. I can say it here, however.

Needless to say, the partner in a relationship that has been ended by another person will have feelings of depression. This is because they have lost somebody that they wanted. There is a loss of hope in restoring the relationship and of ever having another that is successful. They will blame themselves and search for reasons. This process will drag up every dark thought in their psyches. You will have the equivalent of an emotional hangover. It passes. Be patient and be resolved to be rid of the thing that blighted your life.

Keep this in your head. **'I deserve better than this'.** Make it your secret mantra and repeat over and over in your mind.

The narcissist became your addiction. Like many drugs, it was pleasant at first but then became a vital part of your life. You are going to kick the habit. It will possibly take time but once you start to stop needing it, then you are moving forward in the right direction.

If you give in to his demands then be prepared to be treated like an animal in quarantine. Family and friends are a threat to the narcissist's control. Yet here lays a solution. Take the bull by the horns. Be like you were before. Talk to others. You have nothing to lose but the monster in your life.

It is as if they are an alien species in a sci-fi horror film, bent on the destruction of human happiness and whose aim is to reduce good feelings to dust.

Back to myths. Dracula was a brute who sucked the blood and lifeforce out of his victims. He was a representation of the narcissists we know about today.

He was charming during the day when hiding from the sun but when the dark night came in then, disappearing into the shadows, he was the predator of innocence. Thankfully, he was always outsmarted by the hero. The heroes in your life are yourself, your family, friends and counsellors who will help and protect you. When that sun shines again, then the vampire is reduced to ash, to nothing.

You are the one who needs to escape. Just picture this; you have been trapped in a dark cave by a monster who lured you in by being charming, handsome(?), caring, in need of your help and understanding. He looked like a movie idol at first but became the star of a horror film.

You have good memories of what life was like before the s*** hit the fan. Go back to those memories, remember being free from hassle, threats, abuse, pain and emotional grief.

When you first walk out of the cave the sunlight hurts your eyes. You are feeling in a panic and want to rush back to the cavern. Yet, after a short while, your eyes get used to the light and you can look around at the beautiful scenery full of the family and friends you were forced to push away, but who still love you because they understand what you have been through.

Withdrawing. When you hold back from giving what is wanted then he is in a difficult situation.

They are weak, as already said, which is why they have to do what they do to try to demolish you so they can feel strong. It is part of their delusion; they are still weak. Narcissists are not happy by nature because they cannot accept themselves and others as they really are.

The Mirror Image. It is almost certain that when the parting is imminent or when it happens, you will be the subject of an avalanche if insults, name calling and accusations. Why does this happen?

Simply put, you have been his reflection that Narcissus fell in love with. He has realised that it is not a perfect mirror image of himself anymore. What Narcissus had was just what he wanted to see and hear. He had control but when his reflected self did not seem to love him back unconditionally, he smacked the water, swore at the reversed picture of himself in his attempts to be idolised.

What the narcissistic controller is doing by shouting at you, by being accusing, by being threatening is actually him screaming at himself.

All of what he says is an actual manifestation of his own, but unaccepted, weakness that at some level of his mind he knows, but will never confess consciously.

In brief, his insults are a reflection of him, not you.

Cutting contact. Make sure that you build a barricade of silence. When you make the break then he will want to goad you, encourage you to come back. He wants you to admit defeat and beg for his return to your life. Just as sure as he used methods to gather you, he will have access to a new battery of techniques to attempt to wear you down.

You are unable to put him in a cage, and you need to avoid isolating yourself. You were confined for too long by him.

Make contact with friends and family to explain what has happened. They **WILL** help you because they want you back in their lives and you will discover that they worried about your safety and wellbeing without criticism.

Cut all ties with your jailer. Block him on social media and on your phone, put his email address into junk. Do everything you can to prevent him from bothering you. If you had just escaped from a quicksand then there is absolutely no reason to get back in to test if it is safe. It will still suck you down in order to get you back as his whipping boy, or girl.

You also need to remove photos that you have of him. He was your bad dream, your nightmare, and you have no reason to be reminded of it.

It will make you weak if you think about the past. Your mind will become selective and remember the few good times at the expense of ignoring the many bad ones. Avoid thinking about him in everyway.

Ditto for mementos and other things that were deliberately placed to help him in the eventuality that you left his life.

Remember good times with friends and family. Recall what life was like before you became infected by the narcissistic virus that he spread.

WARNING. THEY CAN RETURN AS DIFFERENT PEOPLE !

I will put this as directly as I can. Once you get rid of one narcissist, then you will find yourself attracted to others.

The reason is that you parted from the one before on bad terms. You could well be feeling worthless and stupid at having been caught, (which you were not, by the way) and you are vulnerable. You want the security of true love and the new love bomber will find you easy prey, **UNLESS,** you make sure you are prepared to recover before going back into a relationship.

Choose the new person in your life like you are buying something precious. Do it slowly. Check its background, think about the approach and whether or not the signs of a predator are there. Repeat, if its too good to be true, then it probably is.

For a period of time your emotions will be like a hermit crab between shells. Soft, vulnerable and easy to catch and consume. You have to place your emotions in a hard shell that will enable you both to see and protect yourself from the seagulls who are always looking for sustenance.

Be careful. Talk about possibilities to friends and if they grill you, be happy and grateful because they will help you.

Any new partner in your life who is worthy of you will have a totally different approach to the one before. He will be more patient, probably less romantic and demanding, it is true. Nice people are much more transparent.

TIME FOR A BREAK 4

Let's recap the main points.

1. You need him to reject you for good rather than just falling into his trap of you missing him and begging for his return. This is for your benefit rather than his.

2. It is essential that you break contact permanently.

3. Get help by contacting the friends and family that you were forced to dismiss from your life. They will understand, sympathise and help you. Just because you ignored them, they still feel warmly about you, especially when you explain. Nothing to be embarrassed about. It happens to many, many people.

4. Beware of a fast replacement by somebody who is ready to take advantage.

RECOVERING YOUR LIFE

Springing Back

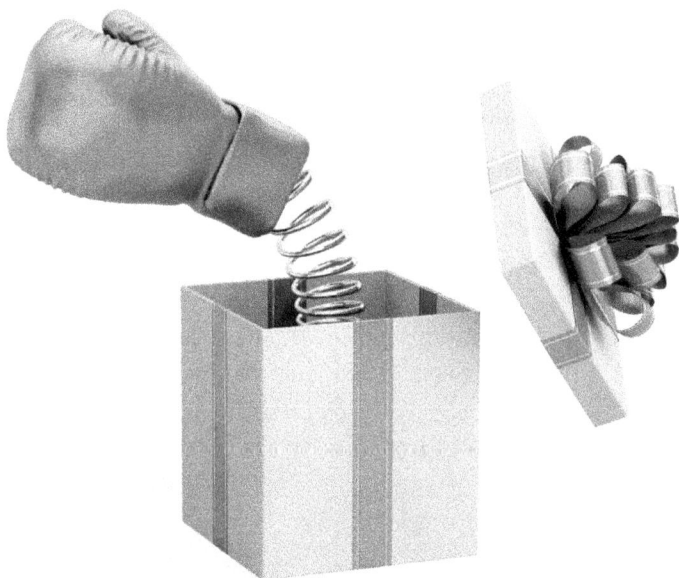

This is a very important part of this book. Rather than offering advice such as, leave him. That is too easy to say but difficult to do.

This will show you tried and tested methods to become the free person you were before being trapped.

And please, stop trying to analyse him or yourself before or after you get rid of him. You did nothing wrong. You were far from being a vulnerable idiot, you were caught by one of the best predators in the business.

Think of a metal spring in a Jack-in-a-box. You have been compressed by the weight of his attention, his self-pity, his open or subtle bullying.

Now, when that weight is lifted, the spring expands to be what is was before, but with a boxing glove for protection rather than for attacking!

That is you, but you are now stronger than you were before and you can use the bounce to push away any attempts to flatten you again.

You will now build your confidence and self-belief back to where it should be. Your life is not dependant upon another, an emotional leech. All that he said to you, nice or nasty, was a bunch of lies told for his benefit.

Good riddance to bad rubbish.

PTSD

Post Traumatic Stress Disorder, which we will call Post Narcissist Stress just to make it easier to deal with.

You have been traumatised by the lies, insults, buttering up and being made to feel inferior. Getting away involves more than just leaving. The survivors have to deal with the mess in their minds. There are also the issues that he carries with him. He thinks he still owns you and that you have made a big mistake in getting rid of him.

This means he might engage in something called **hoovering** where he wants to pick up the pieces of you that are broken by the loss of love and care you thought, erroneously, that you had. The only love in the relationship was his for himself. You were only there to boost his ego, to be his emotional slave and to please him even when you were being shouted at, criticised and hurt emotionally and perhaps physically.

He needs his supply and you have to, and absolutely must, deny him any contact where his claws might grip you again. He remains the devious man he always was.

Talk about what happened to your family and friends you still have friends and a loving family even though they feel that they have been rejected by you for no reason. Believe it or not, **EXPLAIN** what the reasons were, how you were caught hook, line and sinker by a skilled hunter. There is no embarrassment in telling your story, there are so many others just like yours. You will discover that when they know the truth, they will be there to support and help you in a sympathetic way. If you attempt to go it alone, then you might be so lonely that you could just feel that the trap you were in is worth getting back into. That would be your gravest peril to do.

The most effective therapy for PTSD is talking about what happened, maybe to a counsellor or therapist. Sometimes the memories are painful to recall but what is happening is a change of context. What happened was in the past and in the telling, the effects are diluted bit by bit until the trauma can be understood and lived with.

TALK it through with somebody, anybody other than the person you have escaped from. Most importantly, forgive yourself. You were the innocent victim of a well practised hunter of a suitable quarry for HIS needs.

Self-Reliance, Believing In You

This is aimed at changing your mindset from helping him to get better, to again become the loving and caring man you first met. You could well believe that you caused him to change, that he is really the charmer but, being with you damaged him.

Narcissism is a mental disorder than cannot be cured. He is stuck with it but there is no reason why you should be stuck with him.

He was a monster from day one. Well camouflaged, cloaked and disguised for the soul purpose of finding somebody who would feed his need for admiration. You never changed him, he was always like that and will never get better. He was and is the leech that needed the equivalent of blood, your devotion to an ever changing person who pushed you to the limits and beyond. The more you gave, the more he took until you felt too weak to fight back.

Now you are going to find the strength that is in you, but was suppressed by fear. Remember Popeye. When he was weak and on the point of defeat, he would squeeze the can of spinach and eat its contents. Suddenly he was a strong person again and able to fight back and win. That metaphor is about your inner spirit that just needs to be found and used to get the strength to do what you have to do.

And if you wonder if you are the only, or just one of a few who have been caught and used, think back to children's tales that were based on abuse of the individual.

Rapunzel locked in a tower.

Little Red Riding Hood who was attracted by somebody she thought she loved, her grandmother, but it was in fact a hungry and needy wolf like your narcissist.

Snow White was nearly killed by her narcissistic step-mother, but was revived when she spat out the piece of poisoned apple stuck in her throat.

There are so many that give warnings about predators disguised as benevolent people. The wolf is a beautiful animal but when it is hunting, it is dangerous. That is why it appears in so many stories such as the Werewolf.

You were a victim but you are not stupid, far from it. And you are just one of many thousands who have been caught by the cunning thieves of innocent people.

The following has been taken from my book, **STOP BELIEVING THE LIES, BELIEVE IN YOURSELF**. It has been amended to target the needs of a recovering victim.

And to help you, from now on, the word survivor will replace victim.

Changing your Language and Your Thinking

THIS PART IS EXTREMELY IMPORTANT. BECAUSE WE TAKE OUR LANGUAGE PATTERNS FOR GRANTED.

PLEASE. TAKE IT SLOWLY. THE BENEFITS ARE ENORMOUS.

WHEN WE THINK, it is like having a conversation within our own minds. This is our internal dialogue. Those thoughts are 'flavoured' by our emotions. We run a process of risk evaluation at the same time. When we are walking, we recognise ruts in the road, or dark corners where dangers might lurk. However, when we worry, we think about problems that might become reality without having rational justification.

We know that our thoughts can change our feelings. Fear is an emotion. Those fears that seem to come from nowhere have their origins in our unconscious thoughts rather than from a recognised stimulus. We react as if the threat were a real thing. Rather than thoughts they become 'feelings.' Yet when those thoughts are of pleasure, we relax.

The language that we use for our internal and external dialogue is important for our well-being and for dealing with the problems that underlie our anxieties and lack of self-belief. Within modern culture there are four things relating to language which work against us, but which we can use to our advantage when we know the secrets.

1. We live in a society that sells problems for a living.
Can you imagine taking your car to a showroom where you are told that the vehicle you have is perfect? No! They might suggest that the mileage is high, or the engine size is unsuitable, or that the fuel consumption is uneconomical. They will identify and explain the 'problems' that you have and then they will solve them by selling you a new car. This applies to most trades.

Even salaries are paid because if your position were vacant, the company would have a problem in getting its necessary work done. We survive by solving problems, and then by maintaining the possibility of the problem recurring.

Now you have got this far, you are solving your problem for good. If you are careful in the future then the possibility of it recurring will be eliminated.

You may well have been attracted to the narcissist because you were lonely and he offered to solve that problem by giving you the moon. Then you discovered that one simple problem had been replaced by another that was far bigger and dangerous to your wellbeing.

2. We use words too cheaply.
We sustain our personal problems by the poor use of language. That is, we use words too cheaply. We pepper our speech with brief idioms that communicate on a superficial level, but have different deep-seated meanings. My favourite example of poor language that is counter-productive came from a client who said: "Perhaps I really ought to try to think more positively!" That sentence contained all the reasons why she would find it difficult to do so.

So, how about, "I really need to remove the cause of my issues, this man, from my life". **NO,** instead, "I am solving my problems by being strong and by thinking in a new way".

The words 'perhaps', 'I really', 'ought' and 'try' are weak rather than positive. They are 'failure' words. They appear to state a positive objective but they infer that the goal will be missed. If the intention is firm then the sentence becomes, "I think positively" and "I am solving my problem by removing the cause."

3. We like negatives!

We tend to use strange constructions that are based on double negation. Why do we say, "that's not a bad idea" rather than "that's a good idea", for example?

Negatives are necessary for rational disciplines. Mathematics has to have the concept of negatives to work, but we are dealing with our emotions. As you will see later, negatives are unable to dismiss problems but they potentially intensify them.

4. We make our lives conditional.

We make statements to ourselves and then accept them as solid truths. Superstitions are a good example. "If I walk under a ladder then I will be unlucky" or "a black cat crossing my path is a good omen" or a bad one in some cultures! We make our lives conditional. If X happens then Y will follow.

This happens with anxiety states. "If I go to the supermarket then I will have a panic attack." I have even heard the statement, "I know that I will get a panic attack two and a half hours after taking my beta-blocker." Surprise,

surprise! She did until we changed her language.

"If I remove him from my life then he will be unhappy." (Will he?)

"If I get rid of him then I will miss the person who once made me so happy." (Will you?)

"If we separate then he will not love me anymore." Sorry, but he never did. He loves himself.

Suggestions are quickly made and adhered to. When we make the wrong choices with suggestions then we pay the price.

So now we are going to sort them out.

Breaking Out of Thinking Traps

Our self-talk is full of traps. Most people have heard of the word **'affirmation'**, a positive phrase or suggestion aimed at changing the ways in which we think about ourselves. The most famous one is "Everyday, in every way, I am getting better and better."

However, very few people actually use positive affirmations. Most of us are very adept at using negative ones by accident! We develop and hold onto erroneous beliefs that distort and change our behaviours and attitudes.

Sadly, we are wonderful in reinforcing negatives by our thinking. When we make negative suggestions to ourselves then we run a huge risk of believing them. Things like the following need to be ruthlessly destroyed. "I am unlucky", "I am ugly", "I am a loser", "I will get fired because I am useless at my job," "I deserved being involved with a narcissist because I am a loser."

There is a way to break the negativity of our self-talk. We use very positive techniques for changing our language, which in turn modify our thinking, emotions and reactions. These are based on eliminating negative words and conditions. We replace them with a language and thinking that contains beneficial intention and positive intent.

The rules and steps are simple and easy to remember.

Look at the sentence **'I will NOT panic** (or not get

angry/become anxious/get stressed, etc.) **in the supermarket'** (or in the car, at the restaurant, at work, on a date, etc.) This seems as if it will work.

However, within that short sentence there are three fundamental errors of thought that will bring about the opposite response. From working through this example, we see how to turn our goals into language that communicates the correct message to our minds.

1. 'I WILL' puts the hoped-for solution into the future. The future is tomorrow, next week, next year, whatever. This tells us that whereas relief will be found, it is unlikely that it will help us <u>now</u>. Putting that hope into the future reinforces the problem that you currently have. It becomes a self-fulfilling prophesy.

The first rule and step is to place your problem into the past tense.

If it WAS a problem, then it follows that it has gone. Your mind gives you the unconscious positive suggestion, or affirmation, that you need. You put the solution into the present tense by using the words 'I' and 'NOW'.

The affirmation then becomes: 'I **used** to panic in the supermarket (or whatever) **BUT NOW, I feel peaceful, safe and relaxed.**'

And for you, 'I was ensnared by a nasty man **BUT NOW, I am free from all of that heartache and grief that he caused.**'

If you find that your mind tells you that your problem still exists, then argue with it! Repeat your affirmation over and over.

2. The second rule is to lose the small word **'NOT'** in suggestions. (It works in prose but is a no-no in self-talk. Although we know what positive suggestions are, we fail to use them. Instead, anxiety sufferers use negative suggestions accidentally. These maintain the problem rather than giving a solution. When we are thinking about behaviours, our minds seem to be unable to recognise negatives. When we use the word 'NOT' we often create the opposite outcome to that which is desired. Let me give an example: **'Do NOT think of blue elephants!'**

It is likely that you thought of blue elephants. It therefore follows that the sentence 'I will NOT panic in the supermarket' is understood as 'I WILL panic in the supermarket' because the instruction is contained after the word 'NOT' in the words 'panic in the supermarket'. The word 'not' has no effect in changing that instruction. The blue elephant example told you, after the word 'NOT', to **think of blue elephants.**

Use a sentence that affirms what you want to happen rather than using a negative in an attempt to negate the unwanted effect. To repeat, lose the word 'NOT' from your thoughts. To replace it state the result that you want in positive terms.

A quick note. Whereas the word 'not' is to be avoided in suggestions and self-talk dialogue, it is permitted in negating things as in 'blue is not green'. And, people who tell me I am stupid, ugly, etc are not nice.

3. The third rule, and next step, is to omit any reference to the problem when you are used to putting it into the past and when you have stopped using the word 'not'. The last part of the sentence is a reminder of the problem and it is emphasised. '...panic in the supermarket.' It tells you to do what you want to avoid. Never feed a problem by talking or thinking about it. Starve it to death. Make it an exile, something that used to cause upsets but which has now been eliminated. Eliminate the problem and tell yourself what you want to happen. 'In the supermarket (or in the car, at the restaurant, at work, on a date, etc.), I am calm, confident and in control.

PUTTING IT ALL TOGETHER:

1. Make your suggestions positive, current and relevant to the solution. Ignore the problem completely. It is something that you used to have, but now you are fine.

2. Avoid certain other words such as 'perhaps', 'ought', 'should', 'maybe', 'if', 'might', 'probably' and 'try'. These imply either failure or weakness.

3. Make your internal dialogue strong and assertive. Tell yourself what you want to be by telling yourself that what you once wanted in the future is how you actually are, **now**.

4. To summarise, model your suggestion on the following, "In the supermarket I am calm, peaceful and relaxed." Stop your language from telling you otherwise.

Can you now see why 'DON'T PANIC' is the WORST thing to say in a crisis? 'STAY CALM AND RELAXED' is so much better.

Write down your first thoughts about how you would like to feel. Now review what you have written and edit it to eliminate the words that affirm your problem. Rewrite your aims in positive words that contain the solution in the present tense. Check your words with the lists given a little later in this chapter.

I AM CALM, CONFIDENT AND IN CONTROL is your new motto. It sums up everything that you wanted and what you are **NOW.**

Become your own editor.

Editors check the constructions of words and grammar before publication. When you think, check how you are thinking. Your objective is to ensure that your thinking and spoken words are positive and direct. Delete any negatives that you find in your inner and outer dialogues.

Two negatives do not make a positive! Yes! I have used the 'not' word. As written above, using the word 'not' in a sentence with positive intent reverses the meaning. However, attempts to change a negative sentence into a positive one are ineffective.

To demonstrate this, it is better to give an example. If we use the sentence "I will not stay calm" rather than "I will not panic" then they will both have the same effect of signalling alarm. That little word is a negative influence whichever way you look at it! Throw it away. Refuse to use it. This becomes easier with time, I promise.

Read, watch and listen to advertisements.

Good advertising copywriters are skilled people who have to communicate messages which will evoke positive action. They sell the benefits of a product or service. You will notice the absence of weak words such as 'try', 'don't', 'won't'. However, notice the abundance of affirmative words such as 'will', 'can' and 'now'. Make sure that you analyse high quality advertisements. The most adept advertising professionals will have written these. Make a list of the active and optimistic words and add them to your vocabulary. Compare them to advertisements in local newspapers from small businesses. There you will spot the less effective use of language. Remember that advertisers are setting up needs to be resolved by you purchasing the product or service that settles the need you were unaware of before.

As a quick note, during the love bombing stage, you were sold to by an expert in the use of magnetic wording. That was from his experience with many of his prey before you.

Some of you will be thinking that the word 'try' is used in advertising. 'Try our product and if you do not like it, get your money back.' This works on the idea that when you try something then the bother to get the money back will put people off making the effort. Here the word try invites people to test. It implies that the manufacturer has confidence. It probably has an effect. The manufacturers think the risk is worth taking because we enjoy receiving but dislike the effort of returning something.

However, 'try to lose weight with our product' is different. Here the failure sense would be implied as happens in most cases of the use of the word. In short, lose the 'try' word!

When the coercive controller, love bomber or narcissist

tells you he will 'try' to get better, then that is one of the few times that he is telling you that he a failure. He misunderstands the true meaning of the word as non-fulfilment.

Listen to politicians. (Yes. Narcissists can be useful at a good distance!)

Politicians sell voters the apparent problems caused by their oppositions and then they offer the solutions that they think that they have. Watch news programmes to explore the language used. Notice the cryptic meanings of phrases such as 'their employment policy is not working', the hidden emphasis being on 'is not working' suggesting that there will be unemployment. The follow up would be 'our employment policy will bring rich rewards to our voters'. Remember that our culture sells solutions to problems that we create. Politicians are coached in the use of language by experts behind the scenes. Their speeches are scripted rather than heart-felt in lots of cases.

Listen to positive people.

Listen to the words and expressions of people who are NORMAL and confident. Their self-esteem is reflected in the language that they use with others. It follows that their internal dialogue is as assured as their outward speech.

WORDS, WORDS AND WORDS TO AVOID

Try. Implies failure. Remember that when somebody says that they will try to see you at 3 o'clock, that gives you at least ten more minutes before they will actually arrive.

Not. Creates a negative suggestion as already mentioned.

But. When used in the present tense to explain why something will fail. In this way, 'but' creates the negative

69

reinforcement of the problem. For example, "I would like to drive on motorways, but I panic."

Perhaps. Conditional expectation of failure as in "perhaps I will get better".

Might. Conditional expectation of failure as above.

Maybe. Conditional expectation of failure as above.

Should. Conditional expectation of failure as above.

WORDS TO USE CAUTIOUSLY

All words which put action or intent into the future. They maintain the problem in the present time. However, if they reflect an intent that was previously missing and a time frame, they are useful. For example, "I will go to the doctor tomorrow" or "I can relax when I visit the hairdresser in an hour's time."

Can. A positive word that refers to the future but is sometimes conditional.

Will. A positive word that refers to the future.

If. This makes the intent conditional. An example of bad usage is, "if I meet somebody new, then I will be anxious." An example of better usage is, "if I use positive language then I will be in control." However, it is best to say, "I use positive language and I am in control, now." (See below.)

WORDS TO USE

70

(I) **Do.** A positive word in the present time.

(I) **Am**. A positive word in the present time.

Now. A positive word in the present time.

But (when following placing the problem into the past tense.) Used this way, 'but' creates a positive affirmation. For example, "I used to worry about how bad I might be when we separate, but now I feel happy, calm, confident and in control."

Avoid. This is a word of positive intent. "I used to get angry with myself, but now I avoid criticising myself by recognising my true value."

As. A conditional word that implies a result. For example, as you read this book you find it is helping you to improve your life.

FOLLOW THE RULES, PLEASE

Rather than just reading the language rules given above, become familiar with them, understand them and then adopt them.

THEY ARE:

1. Place your problem into the past tense and the positive outcome in the 'here-and-now'.
2. Lose the word 'not', and any other 'weak' words.
3. Then, omit any reference to the problem. Define the solution in 'strong' words.

**REMEMBER,   AS   YOU   CHANGE   THE
LANGUAGE OF YOUR THOUGHTS, THEN:**

**Your mind becomes more relaxed;
Then your body posture changes;
Then your breathing changes;
Then your life changes...for the better.**

Relaxation And Coping

Like me, you will have received numerous emails selling the greatest relaxation techniques ever, for scary prices. Forget the snake-oil salesmen. They are spinning the same lines as the love bomber.

Relaxing is part of our nature. We do it when we are asleep and we do it naturally when our minds are at peace.

LEARNING TO RELAX is straightforward. Making the time to relax on a regular basis is the thing which causes the most problems for people. It is easy to write that you should meditate for ten minutes in the morning and for twenty minutes in the evening. People with that much time to spare should be stress-free in any event!

Therefore, the following is a realistic approach to relaxation for people who have little time to spare. This can be done within any time-frame and in any location which is safe.

When you are relaxed, repeat positive suggestions and your affirmations over and over in your mind. Use your imagination. The relaxed feelings that you have, open the door to your unconscious mind and you have now the language to communicate with it.

"EASY-MEDITATION."

Rather than to achieve a state of nirvana, our aim is to experience the calm, confident and in control state on a regular basis in order to reduce anxiety and self-deprecation.

Hence the name.

Getting ready. Find the most suitable place that you can. It might be an armchair, settee, bed or the floor. Equally, due to circumstances, it might be a railway carriage, your office or your car-seat in a rest stop. There should be no rules for relaxation, or time limits. Tailor your resources to your circumstances.

HOWEVER, NEVER DO THIS WHEN DRIVING.

The basics.
Make yourself comfortable and safe. If you are using your car whilst parked up, for example, lock the doors. If you are in a train, ensure that any valuables that you have are secure.

Positioning.
Sit or lay in such a way that your body is as open as the surroundings and decency permit.

The tradition meditation position where you sit on the floor with your legs in the lotus-position is fine if you can put up with the discomfort! However, just sitting with the soles of your feet together and your knees as far apart as possible opens up the pelvic area and encourages deep abdominal breathing almost automatically. If you sit on the floor with your legs together and outstretched, you will notice how much this restricts your ability to breathe into your stomach.

When you lay or recline, make yourself as open as you are able.

Run a muscle-check. Relax your neck, shoulders and stomach. Ease out the thigh and calf muscles. Separate your ankles and open your legs as much as your situation allows. Let your arms droop down or rest them on your thighs. Open your hands.

USING YOUR SIX SENSES.

1. Proprioception (or mental massage)
This is the sense that we are least familiar with by name, but we know what it is when explained. It is the sense that, amongst other things, will know where the light switch is in the dark. It is an awareness of where parts of you are in space.

Start with the top of your head and work down to your feet. All animals prefer to be stroked downwards than upwards. Do it to your dog or cat. You will notice a difference. Concentrate on breathing slowly into your abdomen. Ignore your upper chest. That will fill on its own.

Feel, with your mind, every part of your head every time you breathe in. As you breathe out say to yourself, **"I am calm, confident and in control, now."** Or whatever positive thing you want to say to yourself.

Feel, with your mind, each part of your head including your hair, ears and nose as well as the muscles. Move down your body doing the same thing, in whichever order you like, but include every part of you. You will finish with your toes. When you get there enjoy the feeling and, if you wish, include one or more of your other senses.

2. Visualisation.

Imagine whatever gives you pleasure; a beach, a waterfall, swimming with dolphins or a person other than the one you want out of your life. Anything! Imagine it as a picture or as a film. Involve yourself in the scene or watch it as an observer.

3. Hearing.
Listen to imagined birdsong or waves or add your favourite music as a soundtrack. If you are travelling, listen to the rhythm of the train wheels.

4. Smelling.
Smell anything that you can. Imagine freshly cut grass, perfumes or flowers. To some, the smell of a wet dog is relaxing. Alternatively, smell the real odours around you.

5. Tasting.
Add a favourite meal or the taste of a blade of grass in your mouth.

6. Feeling.
This is the sense of feeling the world outside of us. The textures, temperatures and shapes of things, real or imaginary.

This process of focusing thoughts onto pleasant things takes us away from the worries that haunt anxious people and puts us into a safe environment where the calm, confident and in control state takes over. You relax for as long you have time to do so. For some it will be twenty minutes, for others two. There are no rules. The only thing that is important is that you do it.

RELAXING WITH REAL EXPERIENCES

Our memories work with associations, so concentrate on positive ones from before your personal crisis.

The above exercise brings about relaxation by using the imagination with associations. We can reverse the process by using real objects to stimulate pleasant memories of relaxing events. The following are examples of things that may be used to help relaxation.

1. Proprioception.
This can be anything from dancing to Tai Chi. Movement is relaxing. Feel, with your mind, where your limbs are located in space when you move.

2. Visualising.
Look at landscapes, pictures or photographs that have pleasant connotations. Draw, even if you feel that you lack the talent.

3. Hearing.
Listen to recordings that inspire images. Listen to music, birdsong or wind-chimes. Hear children laughing. Listen to what appears to be silence and find sounds within it.

4. Smelling.
Gently sniff foods, spices, flowers. Grade them. Find categories and rank them in order of preference.

5. Tasting.
Roll foodstuffs and drinks around in your mouth like a gourmet or wine taster. Define the differences between sweet and sour. Determine the ingredients used in the things

that you eat.

6. Feeling.

Touch and feel the different textures of cloth or modelling clay. Feel the different wall coverings in your house. Caress plants and/or pets.

ROLE MODELLING

Become a method actor. Pretend that you are acting out the role of a confident person, free of stress and problems. You find role models everywhere. There are people that you admire. Copy their posture, their ways of walking, talking and breathing. You find them in real life, television and films. Watch politicians making speeches.

Admire actors in demanding parts. These successful types are acting out their lives. They were born in the same way as you and me, but they have dressed themselves in the behavioural costumes of what they want to portray.

Do the same. What happens is that the fantasy gives an escape from the negative way in which you regarded yourself. It shows you that when you act a character, you become that style of person. You give yourself positive experiences, which you can grow from. You change your approach from running and hiding to that of control of yourself.

The main essence of relaxation is that of occupying the conscious mind to the extent where it stops from being judgemental about the suggestions you want to pass to your unconscious.

Prepare suggestions carefully and make them when you feel relaxed and receptive. It is as if you make yourself an observer sitting in a room while you talk to a confidante, free from interruption or interference.

Finding Contentment

THE PARALLEL UNIVERSE IN YOUR MIND

A parallel universe is just in the imagination, isn't it? It is a place where things are as you wish them to be.

If there is such a place, we should ask the question "Why are those lucky so-and-sos having all the fun?"

Too mystical, yet your mind seems to make your world turn out to be the way you create it. The rich always have money because that is the way they see their lives being. Happy people seem to find happiness in their lives because they want it.

So, does a parallel universe really exist? Who knows? There are theories in physics involving protons, neutrons and string theory that are only in the minds of physicists. But there is a mental parallel universe that we can all find.

If we want to access this place where everything is better than the one we live in we have to create it in our minds, in our thoughts and then it starts to exist in our reality and begins to affect our day to day lives.

Our thoughts can create the reality in which we live. Negative thoughts will bring negative results. But why?

Remember the old expression, 'be careful what you wish for'. What you tend to look for is what you will find. A man who looks for apples in an orchard will find them hanging from the trees because he looks upwards and forward.

Another who worries about snakes in the grass will miss the apples because he is looking down fearing a bite, but in reality, he will not see any snakes but might imagine he hears a hiss or sees something moving in the grass. The first man walks away happy, the second worried.

The orchard remains the same but the expectations of the two men are so different.

FUNDAMENTAL DIFFERENCES

With people there are two fundamental elements in behaviour.

The first of these is the fundamental nature, the fixed behaviour of somebody that is difficult or impossible to change. The metaphor of a leopard not changing its spots is important because this describes the basic nature of a person who, despite promising change, is actually trying to put on a disguise to gain advantage knowing that the change is short-term. The patterns in the fur and skin of a leopard are cosmetic so any change is only superficial. Even if the patterns are changed by scarring from a fight with a lion or hyena the nature will remain the same. It is the inner core of the big cat that has to transform. Sadly for our villain, that is impossible.

The second fundamental element is essential change. This is where something has happened that has shown the person that the old behaviour is damaging and destructive. This is where the person needs courage to see that the enemy is within, not outside. There is no fight to win but there is peace to be gained.

The person has to recognise the negative behaviours that

81

have caused conflict and then discharge them into the past where they can dilute and disappear. Look to the future to see and feel the peace, love and harmony that is to be gained. Then incorporate that into the present and a fundamental change will have taken place.

Something can happen in the mind, with the emotions. Here it is called catharsis. It takes something powerful enough to bring it about, but it is possible and it is wonderful.

To make those changes, it is necessary to remove the old negative thoughts and behaviours from yourself Then the attractive and transformed 'you' emerges.

How to do that follows on.

Removing Your Baggage

It is said that there are only two causes of misery; having things that you do not want and not having things that you do want.

If you want a happy life, and most of us do, the following will show you how to stop making it unhappy. It will help you to find real contentment in your life.

First of all, we need to identify what your baggage is and where it came from. Have a look at your garbage bins. Some are for waste that needs to be disposed of permanently, things like food that has become mouldy or rotten. Then there are things that can be recycled such as glass, metal cans, some plastics. They have been used and are now unusable as they are, but can be crushed or melted and turned into something of use and value. Some things can be repaired and made good.

Your emotional baggage is like that. Some things are rotten and are unrepairable. They will probably relatc to your experiences in the past. Get rid of them. Some things can be mended or recycled, however.

This book is about dealing with your problems, your need for self-belief, self-esteem and confidence

It is necessary to look through your emotional baggage piece by piece. Yet there is one fundamental thing we need to address as a priority.

Dealing With Memories

He is out of your life, now, but the memory is an ogre that sits in our minds and gets its revenge on us as survivors. When we refer to the good memories we are tempted to feel sorry for him and maybe he can still be rescued, but then we mess up our lives in terms of guilt.

No, the memory has to be renamed as the little s*** that lives in our heads and has tantrums and makes us have tantrums as well, while it laughs at our misery.

It is perhaps what invited the monster into your life to continue its path of destruction in the first place. It was not you but, hey, there is nobody else other than you and the people you loved and it got its kicks from by screwing you up.

You cannot change the past, it is true, but you can prevent yourself from being reminded of the past. If you shout or swear at somebody, especially those that you love, then you are taking out the payback of the ogre on somebody else. The more you hurt those people then the happier that tyrant becomes. That feeling of anger at others is part of the legacy he has left behind. When that monster goes out of your life then you revert to the way you should be and you are left with no regrets.

Allow yourself to be the mature grown up that you are. His destructive childish behaviour was part of his attempts to destroy your relationships, and eventually you. Those memories can do nothing but hurt you now.

Be bold, get rid of the beast inside your mind. It exists no more than your childhood goldfish that died and was buried or flushed down the toilet.

THE VENTRILOQUIST'S DUMMY

The malevolent ventriloquist's dummy is a great metaphor for the narcissist. It sits next to a person and says outrageous things, swears and has an attitude of superiority to the person who is working it. People laugh at the embarrassment caused to the operator. Because it is removed as a source of pain to the audience, the onlookers love it all. Of course, the dummy needs somebody to work it, and to care for it without returning much at all.

If you want examples, watch or read the plots of great films such as Magic with Anthony Hopkins where the dummy, Fats, takes over the consciousness of the ventriloquist and ruins his existence.

Let us call this memory of the beast Dummy, because you cannot see it but it is part of you but it seems impossible to get hold of and remove. It is a part of you that encourages you to be remorseful and alone. More of Dummy later.

The story of dummies creating hurt is reproduced in many films. The spiteful dummy is a physical representation of the memories left by nasty and malicious natures of some people. It wants conditional love and a million other things.

Tantrums and threats work for them. A tantrum gets loads of negative attention. Attention is what they want whether negative or positive. Of course, when the tantrum stops they get positive attention as the relief kicks in. It is like stopping banging your head against a wall. It feels better when you give it a break.

Threats are things like telling a partner how much they hate them and they will threaten to do something bad unless they get what they want. What they want is attention.

Compare the above to a cat that sits on your lap and for no reason scratches you and runs away. When it wants food again it will sit on your lap and purr for attention and because it is being sweet and nice, it will get what it wants.

The great image to create to get rid of those experiences that still control your life is that of separation of two elements; you as you **are**, and you as you **were**.

In your mind either throw the ventriloquist's dummy into the crusher or take it to bits and recycle the parts into something useful and helpful to your life.

The other way to look at your dummy is as the 'monkey on your back'. Getting it off is an expression that says get rid of your problems by taking control of your life without interference from a monkey hindering what you want.

If you are worried that there are too many mixed metaphors, Monkeys and the Ventriloquist Dummy, these are used to expand the point that the something that haunts us needs to be eliminated.

That is history. You are the only person who decides how to act in the present part of your life. You cannot change the past but it can show you what to avoid. Remove your history as a model for how to behave. You are no longer that victim who lives in your memory, but you are now a survivor who has a better life to look forward to.

WRITE A STORY

It sometimes helps if you write a story about a fictional person who got captured and then escaped from a narcissist. Explain how it was done, how your heroine got over the withdrawal and how life got better. Rather than being fiction, you will find that you have written your own way to cope and win.

Dealing With The Dummy

You might be saying that your mind is already occupied with thoughts about him. Now we shall run through an exercise to change your mind and to prevent the past from spoiling your life in the future.

DEALING WITH THE DUMMY

OK, this sounds bizarre but please trust me. It works.

We referred to the removal of the vindictive Dummy the personal ventriloquist's dummy who made us into the sad person who has suffered hurt and heartbreak as a result. Remember that those earlier influences of love, support and warmth will remain.

As an aid, think of your life as a nice garden pond full of pretty fish that represent your good memories. Then, out of the blue a piranha appears and starts to devour them one by one and every time you introduce a new happy memory from the present time, that gets eaten too. Simple solution, remove the piranha and allow the life in your pond to flourish.

We will visualise an outcome.

Read through the following and then copy the process in whichever way you can, in your mind. You should be in a comfortable position, breathing gently and with closed eyes. There are no rules, just be at peace.

Imagine that you can see all of the negative factors in

your life, those things that have been said and done to you.

Then see them as pieces of smashed debris on a smooth and level floor. If you cannot visualise something that is able to be thrown onto the floor then imagine that you are writing that event, hurt or person onto a piece of paper that you can screw up and discard onto the floor.

Dummy, that bad guy, is near you. Break the dummy into bits and throw them onto the floor as well. You might imagine pained, childish noises of protest. You might hear pleading; you might feel sorry for this representation of the man who hurt you. Be strong, ignore everything. It is not a real person; it is an evil life spoiling representation of the causes of your misery made from clay, wood, plastic and cloth with a few mechanical parts. Ideal for recycling.

Now sweep it all up. Vacuum it up if you want, using an industrial scale machine. Hear the cries of pain and hurt he caused. See the tears he made flow, your own and others. Enjoy the silence from Dummy as the fiend is now unable to speak or make a noise.

Put all of this debris into a big hessian sack. Use a dustpan and brush to get every part packed away.

Take it to the trash dump and throw it away.

Relax and feel proud of yourself.

So, Where Is He Now?

What is he doing? Where will he live? Who is he with? Basically, it makes no difference, but you need to keep those thoughts out of your mind.

You need to stop thinking about him. He has gone and you must stop those thoughts by thinking about you and where you are in your life and where you want to be.

That leads to a few issues.

He still thinks that he owns you and feels angry that you have pushed him away because, it shows that you must be as stupid as he has told you that you are. How strange yet remember, there again, that he has a different perspective to other folk who are normal.

This leads to something called **hoovering** where he will want to pick up your pieces that were caused by your decision to remove him. He will offer you a variation or the same love-bombing scenario that he used to catch you in the first place. He has a diverse set of strategies but they boil down to one thing. He wants you to be his devotee, the person who sacrifices everything for the self-loving freak who has no feeling for anybody but himself. He cannot deal with being deserted and will do everything he can to bring the stray back into his domain.

This can include **stalking.** As his property you have no say in how you live your life and he wants, demands, to know where you are and who you are with all the time. This would have happened before the break but afterwards it can continue because he is unable to walk away from his possession, even if he has grabbed somebody else. He wants to be the keeper of his hareem.

Another tactic he will use is **avoidance.** It will be, after a split, that he will avoid any contact with you. That is so you might be jealous that he has found another partner, or, you might worry about his welfare and any illnesses he could have lied to you about, or, he will write to you after a while to explain how much he cares and wants to be with you…absence does not make the heart grow fonder because you are aware that he is a wily and conniving beast. Beware, because like any predator whose prey has escaped, he is lurking in the undergrowth to pounce again when you least expect it.

And he will **swear he has changed.** The leopard has changed its spots. As said earlier, the skin might look different but short of a miracle, the creature will still purr but it is set on stalking and ambush.

He needs your emotional shift from dislike back to admiration. Stop feeling guilty that you have removed his nasty words, actions and behaviour from your life.

For you, life has to be different even after the dramatics, it seems quiet. Treat this as the lull after the storm. The one thing you have to do is write him off.

Write him out of your life for good. The best antidote to a poison is stopping taking it. Think of him as the terrifying monster that made you scared in a film but, now, you have left the cinema. It is unable to get you anymore.

The whole one-sided situation has turned on its head. He is the vulnerable one, he is the person who will never find the love that satisfies him. He will always be disliked and despised for being himself. Never feel sorry for him. He was broken when you met him, and like Humpty Dumpty, can never be put back together again.

Like politicians say, their careers always end in failure; it is likewise for the narcissists.

Take a deep breath smile and relax. You are free.

TIME FOR A BREAK 5

We can pause again for a few moments to recap the main points.

1. **Learn to relax and love yourself. Your self-talk is important because it changes the ways in which you think and act.**

2. **Remove him from your emotions. He hurt you, now it is time to disregard him and move on.**

3. **Be careful because he might not feel that it has ended. In his mind he wants his 'property' back.**

THE OVERVIEW

Narcissists are delusional. They are the lead actors in a play he has written about, and for himself.

He will never get better, you will.

Never forgive him for what he did. It was done on purpose. You would not forgive somebody who raped you, and your mind, emotions and soul were violated.

You were never a fool. You were hunted and caught by a skilled predator who was an expert in baiting traps. And not all predators look the same, some stalk and pounce, some entice.

Through no choice of your own, you were isolated like an animal in quarantine because other people, friends and relatives were seen as a danger to the narcissist's control. You can and should be like you were before this monster came into your life. All you have to lose is the pain and anguish you suffered at their hands.

Their weakness is knowing that you have strength. That is why they want to weaken you. Know that you are unbeatable.

Rather than just thinking that you would be better out of his life, it also works that it is best for you for HIM to be out of YOUR life. A double win.

Occupy your life with positive actions, words and thoughts.

Although you are unable to turn back the hands of time, you can turn yourself around to look at a bright and enjoyable future. He was in the past, leave it that way.

You Survived:
the constant checking
the isolation from your friends and family
the swearing
the threats, the insults
the hurt at being cheated on
the loss of your independence
the emotional and maybe physical cruelty

All he did was to make you stronger as a person. Well done. You are a winner.

You squashed the parasitic mosquito, you pulled the blood sucking leech off your body.

Do Something To Occupy Your Mind

Take up an activity, a hobby. There are so many things you can do depending on where you live.

Out of ideas? Get inspiration from reading, films, the television. Maybe do sport or indulge in writing or painting.

When you are thinking about something then you are ignoring thoughts of him.

REVIEWS

This book has a serious purpose. Hopefully it will help the readers to avoid the traps that are too widely available and which are set by narcissistic predators on dating apps, social media, in the workplace, bars and clubs. It also shows to shake off the chains to recover and grow into the future.

To this end, your review would be helpful to allow readers to see the dangers from a safe viewpoint.

Thank you.

PS. As magicians do not like books that give away their secrets, I am sure that there will be some well disguised criticism. I am far from being worried.

s

www.ingramcontent.com/pod-product-compliance
Lightning Source LLC
Chambersburg PA
CBHW060952040426
42445CB00011B/1116